The Graduate's Gift

Wisdom for the journey ahead

WILLIAM LINDEL

Contents

Foreword

To my daughter, Emily:

Because of you I am immensely grateful. You have given me so much joy and pride. Watching you grow and mature through the years has been such an amazing and enriching experience. I so clearly remember the feeling that I had on the first day of your life. Nothing else really compares to becoming a parent. Holding and looking down upon you in my arms, I couldn't help but consider how much my life was changing from that day forward. At some point, this little baby was going to look at me and call me Dad. I knew that someday you would be looking to me for guidance and protection. The word "Dad" has such tremendous power and that day, for the first time, I could feel the magic and the responsibility intrinsic to my new name. I hoped that simple one-syllable term would, someday, bring rise to warm feelings inside of you; emotions that make you feel protected and make you smile. I still hope that is true.

In a flash, that little baby I held in my arms is preparing for all the things that adulthood brings. I have to wonder, did I do enough as your father? Did we have enough tea parties together? Did I give you enough direction, guidance, and wisdom? Did I instill a strong moral compass? Did I give enough of myself to you? Did I spend enough time with you? What did you learn from watching me? Did I do enough to help you prepare you for the next chapter in your life?

Through the following chapters, I want to pass along just a few of these things that I don't know for sure that I taught you, but I feel are really important. I also want to give a piece of me to take with you when you go. A little something that you can literally carry with you, keep on a shelf, or maybe next to your bed. Maybe a day will come when you miss me a little bit and you can pick up this book and remember how much your Dad loves you.

Introduction

This book contains 12 simple "cheat codes" that will help you find sustainable happiness and success in your next chapter of life. Each cheat code represents a piece of wisdom that has become important to me; therefore some of my descriptions may seem a bit personal, but I wanted to provide insight that is open and authentic . However, try to adapt and apply these cheat codes to your own life. Each of these principles are further illustrated by simple statements emphasized in large print. Giving earnest thought and consideration to each of these pieces of guidance will help you every step of the way no matter what your future holds. This book is designed to be read quickly and understood easily. It doesn't have to be read from front to back, especially after reading it for the first time. When the mood strikes, you can read any given chapter or "cheat code" on any given day, as needed. Take from it what you can, but not every cheat code will be for every single reader. Have fun and enjoy it!

Life is Short

As you embark on this next chapter of life, my first piece of advice to you is whenever you drive by a cemetery, to take notice of the tombstones. Yes, the large rocks that commemorate someone's life that have come and gone. These stones can be more than burial markers and memorials of people's lives. They are great reminders of something of critical importance. The flaw of the young has always been the unwillingness to listen to the old. Old people tell us, but do we listen? They all say it.

Life is short and it goes by quickly.

Please just insert that phrase into your mind and leave it there. You, as a new graduate, have the one thing that other people would kill for: youth. For how much money could someone sell a time machine? Because *life is short and it goes by quickly*, people would pay a fortune for just one use of your time machine. It is very common for people to wish that they could go back and live their lives differently. Having the youth and unbridled potential of a new graduate is just as valuable and powerful as a time machine. You should understand and appreciate what you have at this very point in your life! But owning this time machine, that we call youth, and knowing what to do with it are two separate things.

Learning how to best utilize your youth is the genesis of this book. If you owned a time machine, wouldn't you want to know how to best use it? I have spent much of my adult life focusing on how to be a better version of myself. By reading many books on personal development and listening to hours of podcasts, I have learned a lot from great authors, leaders, and motivational speakers. But what has been even more enriching is the experience of life itself. I have lived nearly 50 years and have put forth a lot of focus and effort on how to do life better than I did the day before. I've always tried to be self-aware and reflect back on my experiences with the question: if I were to do it again, what would I have done differently? What I have found is that there aren't any major shortcuts. The adventure through life can be both arduous and beautiful. What I will give you in this book are just a few small nuggets that I have picked up along the way that can help empower you to persevere through difficulty and uncover some of that beauty along *your* journey.

We each get one life, and just one life. Everyone is gifted with free will and can create their life as they choose. It's very similar to being given some paint and an enormous wall on which to paint a mural; or perhaps a huge easel and canvas. Living each day of your life is akin to using a paint brush and making a few strokes with the brush. In the creation of a colossal painting, you can mess up some strokes, but it doesn't wreck your entire work; life is much the same. In life, your decisions on any given day, within limits, don't wreck your life. You get the next day to try again and perhaps improve what you have done previously.

People like me have already painted much of their life's mural. So, we long for what you have, which is a blank slate, or time machine, to repaint the mural of our lives, from the very beginning. Most people wouldn't go back and change significant choices or happenings in their past, but what you often hear is, "I wish I knew then, what I know now."

At your age, I felt as though much of my life had already been written, but I realize now how wrong I was. It may feel like you are a long way from the start of your life, but you are much closer than you realize. When I was your age, I thought much of my life had already been written, but I now realize how wrong

I was and that I was still at the very beginning. You are at the very precipice of your adult life and you can make it anything you want it to be!

Think of yourself as the most amazing and talented artist with a paint brush in your hand, an assortment of colors and other brushes at your side. You have the opportunity to paint whatever you want on your display of life. Each hour is a new and different stroke of the brush. You choose your color, you choose your brush size, you choose how and where to apply the color. Do you have a vision of what the final painting might look like? You might. Even if you think you do, let me break it to you, it's going to look much different than what you currently envision…for the better.

There are things you can do now, at the outset of your life's "painting", to ensure that when you are on the back side of life, that your painting will be something of beauty. The question to ask yourself now is - What can I do now and throughout the course of this artistry known as life that makes this final product a creation that I can look upon with pride and satisfaction…one that makes me smile?

The first and most important step is to choose your colors and your brushes wisely, *with intention* and not at random chance. This book is intended to help you make wise selections. With proper color and brush selections, the painting will be created with much more ease and grace. You will start painting a masterpiece without ever knowing it.

While it might seem morbid, tombstones remind us, every time we see a graveyard, that life is short, and that we are painting our masterpiece, stroke by stroke, hour by hour, day by day. Therefore, we must make the most of each day by making intentional and thoughtful choices. When you see a grave marker, don't think about death, think about living life to the fullest. Enjoy your time machine but don't waste it!

What do you want
people to say about you
at your funeral?

Be Intentional

Now that we have established that, with abundant youth, you currently possess the most valuable commodity on Earth, what are you going to do about it? How do you begin choosing the proper paint brushes and colors to create this masterpiece? Before you can know how to go about living life in a way that honors its brevity, you should know that just by making intentional choices, you are doing great. Many people just float and flounder through life never actually choosing anything for themselves. They never give any thought about their strategies, goals, attitudes, and mindset. No matter what, by choosing to be someone who takes an active role in determining how you show up each day, you are putting yourself ahead of the game.

Choose how you show up.

Similarly to tombstones, I want you to think about funerals. People come to support the family of the dearly departed, but something else occurs as well. Imagine if all of your life, in the end, is actually made into this painting that we have been discussing. Consider all of your future work experiences, all of the fun and adventure, getting married, parenting your children, becoming a grandparent - all that will make your life. Now imagine it all represented in a painted work of art. At a funeral, each person in attendance views this painting of the recently departed person. They deeply contemplate the aggregate of their interactions with the one who has passed on.

Now imagine *your* funeral. How do you want your painting to be viewed and how do you want it to affect or impact the people that came to honor you? Do you want it to inspire others or create indifference? Your painting will look and feel differently to different people, but what's most important is how *you* want the painting of your life to look. I can promise you that when it's all over for you, nobody will be discussing how much money you made, the car you drove, or how big of a house that you lived in. What people remember is how you made them feel. Kindness, humor, love, service…these are the things that people see when they are contemplating you and your lifetime.

In the end, the most
important thing we leave
behind is the impact we have
had on other people.

If you start with the simple hope of living a life that impacts others in a positive way, then the paintbrush strokes that you apply to the canvas each day, week, month, and year, will flow gently and easily. If you *intentionally* set out to create a masterpiece that delivers inspiration to others, then you will.

Intention is the creative force that transforms your imagination into reality.

But for a recent graduate, this idea may seem a bit unimportant or unrealistic. People your age are naturally more focused on getting things done - achieving and accumulating. College degrees, certifications, well-paying jobs, houses, and cars - these things are the focus, right? This is good. You *should* be focused on those things and I encourage you to achieve your highest possible goals and climb the highest mountains. Go, work, do, find, build, achieve, accumulate, win.

Do it all and live with passion. Give it your very best effort. These accomplishments are the large structures in your life's master painting; they are the outlines of the mountains and trees or the buildings and landmarks. They are the major pieces, large and obvious. For example, she was a teacher, he was a carpenter, she was a doctor, he was a great golfer. Other examples include she had 3 children, she was a wonderful dancer, he was married for 60 years, she loved to go hiking, he loved to go sailing, or she loved horses. We characterize our lives and others with these very broad descriptive phrases. But, there is always more to the story.

When considering *how to* paint any of the aforementioned examples, an artist could use any color, any brush, and could apply any particular style. For example, let's take: He was a great golfer. It's a broad statement. What meaning does it actually hold? Let's dig a little deeper and ask a few questions. Let's analyze this portion of this man's life.

What did golf mean to this person? Why did he play golf? Did he recognize the beauty of a well-manicured fairway? Perhaps he appreciated the sun reflecting orange and yellow upon the morning dew. Did he build strong and intimate relationships through friendly competition? Did he spread laughter and happiness while playing the sport? Did he learn lessons on the golf course that he applied in other areas of his life? Did he use the game to escape stress? Did he leverage his love for the game and the good feelings it created within him to the other areas of his life? Did it make him a better version of himself? Did he make others feel inferior to him because of his great skill? Did he mainly experience enjoyment or frustration while playing? Did he use golf to fill his ego by telling everyone how good he was?

The questions you could ask and answers to them are limitless and make up the specific color and style elements of the "brush strokes" for any of his particular days on the golf course. Certainly, each day was different for this fictional golfer. No two days are exactly the same. So, when we think about the statement: "He was a great golfer", there are billions of different paint colors, lines and shades, that represent all of the many moments that he spent becoming and living as a great golfer.

These are the particulars that you get to choose each and every day of your life. Take one brush stroke individually and it might seem insignificant. But each one is incredibly significant because life is short and it goes by quickly.

You will achieve many great things, but the choices you make that determine the how and why behind your achievements are the true treasure.

Your how and why, not the what, leave your impression on the world. I believe in you and your ability to be thoughtful and intentional in how you approach the fine details of *your* life!

Have you ever been really intentional about how you are approaching each day of your life? If so, how were those days different from the ones that you lived robotically?

Elevate

Imagine standing on an overpass that goes over the top of a busy highway. Now envision the cars racing in both directions below you. Just continue to picture this in your head for a few seconds. What do you hear? What do you smell? How do you feel? You hear the vehicle engines get louder as they get closer and fade as they drive away. You hear the rubber tires on the road. You smell the exhaust floating in the air. You are immersed in this scene. You are there in it and focused on it. You are *experiencing* it. You are truly in the moment, experiencing life fully, with your entire being. This is what I call the *perspective of immersion.*

Now imagine the same scene again. Think about the time of day. Perhaps it's morning rush hour. Consider where most of the people in these cars might be going. To work for the day? Maybe to take their kids to school? Perhaps to a meeting or doctor's appointment. What are these people experiencing during their drives on that morning? Are they listening to music and lifting their mood? Are they listening to political talk radio and furthering their anger? Are they chatting with their children or maybe they are thinking through their day ahead? Perhaps they are feeling deep anxiety and dreading a performance review or some other tough situation.

By asking these questions you are starting to emerge from the perspective of immersion and into a more big-picture point of view, the *perspective of elevation.* This transition is achieved by simply considering the larger context of any given moment or any particular situation. You are using your life's + and -

buttons to change your view settings to mentally and emotionally zoom in and zoom out of a particular situation.

The fictional people that you have imagined in our little scene represent regular, real-life people. They are likely our working demographic, taking their kids to school, rushing to get to work on time, and focusing on the requirements of their job. They are feeling anxious about situations at work such as coworkers that they do not like and bosses that don't understand them. They feel conflicted by the simultaneous pulls of home life and work life. For the most part, everyone in the "rat race", as it used to be called, that you are about to enter, is deeply rooted in the perspective of immersion. They are immersed in their daily lives. World class equestrian Will Faudree once said, "We get so busy rushing from one thing to another, and sometimes we lose sight of why we're doing it at all."

It doesn't necessarily mean that they are "living in the moment". Often, they are not "living in the moment", as we traditionally define that phrase as being very conscious and aware. Quite the contrary is true as most people are living life while being very distracted. They are looking at their phones, thinking ahead to their daily schedule; their meetings; their deadlines, etc.

Living and viewing life from the *perspective of immersion* is absolutely necessary and helpful. Living life from this point of mind will help you accomplish whatever each minute, hour, and day demands of you. But, what you must learn to do is to *elevate* your perspective on a regular basis. Elevating your perspective allows you to actually appreciate each moment for what it is and to more fully "live in the moment".

To illustrate an example, think about a course that you might have to take or have taken, perhaps college algebra. Imagine that you are studying for an upcoming test, but the material is frustrating you. You are having a hard time understanding and computing a particular equation. From the narrow perspective of immersion, you might get to the point that you get so frustrated that you get angry. Maybe you throw something against the wall. You tell yourself that you aren't smart enough to get through the class. You consider dropping out of the class or maybe think about dropping out of college altogether. You are immersed in a singular problem so deeply that you are willing to let this problem sink your entire state of mind and to waste all of the work that you put into that class and possibly all of the work you have put into your education.

This is when making the conscious choice of widening and deepening your lens to the *perspective of elevation* will really help. What if you never get to a point of understanding that particular algebraic equation? Can you still pass the upcoming test, but with a lesser grade? Can you still obtain a reasonable grade in the class? Can you still make it to graduation? Why are you in the algebra class to begin with? Of course, it is because a college math class is a required curriculum to obtain this college degree, in this field of interest of yours, that will benefit you for the rest of your life. You are in this math class because you have a bigger purpose in life. It is because you have a vision of yourself as a successful working professional.

From the perspective of elevation, the "problem" starts to change appearance and shrink in size. It is like looking at something on the ground while you are standing on a tall building. How small do the people and passing cars look from a skyscraper? They look tiny and insignificant. How do people and passing cars look from an airplane? You can't even see them. The problem of a frustrating algebra class itself remains the same, but proper perspective minimizes its potential negative impact on your mindset and motivation.

But, what if the problem is a bigger one? Okay, think about standing right next to an elephant. Yes, he is big. You can't even see all of him at once. Now imagine viewing the same elephant by looking down upon him from a mountain top. The larger the problem, the more the *perspective of elevation* will help you to understand the true nature of the problem. From the mountain, you will be better positioned to find creative solutions. You will be less likely to exaggerate the likelihood of negative outcomes and will be better suited to handle the problem all together. From the perspective of elevation, what appeared to be a problem while in immersion, may actually no longer appear to be a problem at all!

What is important to understand is that the ability to oscillate between immersion and elevation is a superpower that you can keep in your personal toolbox at all times. By simply having the awareness of the superpower of perspective, you will be far better equipped at navigating life's challenges. You will possess an incredibly valuable tool that will help enlighten and empower you to achieve your goals in life and help make your dreams become reality. But, like any other skill, you must *intentionally* choose to employ it. Therefore, you must practice this skill so that it starts to become natural to you. As you paint your life's portrait, consider perspective with each stroke. Immersion or elevation? As you develop your ability to choose and oscillate between perspectives, the most wonderful thing will occur. You will eventually be able to hold both perspectives at once! You can be immersed in the moment of life and elevated above it at the same time.

Be in the moment, and above it.

I have a powerful mental vision for you to consider. Think about a basic dog tie-out setup. You know, when you have a dog that is anchored into the ground with a cable leading off from the anchor point. There is the metal curly-q piece of metal that twists down into the dirt until only a top triangle latch point is left visible. This piece provides a strong stationary base for the cable that attaches to it which stretches about 25 feet or so out to a collar with a roaming dog attached. The dog will indeed roam. He will sniff, he will observe and interact with life as he sees it. He will bark at the delivery driver, he will chase the rabbit, and he will dig in the dirt.

Our canine friend lives life from the perspective of immersion, does he not? He is out there doing his thing. He might experience anxiety, fear, excitement, frustration, joy, and wonder all within a five-minute span. Our dog on the end of this tie-out is a metaphor for us living our daily lives. We will go to school and work, interact with teachers and bosses. We will chase after others and dig into things we enjoy. We naturally immerse ourselves deeply into life.

But remember that the dog is wearing a collar, with a cable that leads back to an anchor point. That curly-q metal rod is deeply inserted into the earth. The dirt, roots, worms and everything not easily visible, which lives below the surface, represents the bigger part of you. This bigger part of you is what truly anchors you. It is your life's purpose and passion. It is your family and home. It is love. It is the type of love that is unbreakable and never-ending, like that which is given from your parents to you. It is the foundation of the amazing person that you are. This sub-surface foundation is so grand that you could never dig to the bottom or find its end. It is cool and enriching. It clears your thoughts and lifts you into the perspective of elevation.

Lastly, imagine yourself as a dog barking at the world, but view the dog, not from its actual location, but instead from the anchored curly-q piece of metal. Imagine yourself as that above-ground triangle piece of the metal tie-out anchor rod. You become an observer of the dog. You can see and hear your dog barking at the far end of the 25 feet of cable. That dog represents your immersed self: your school, work, relationships, deadlines, questions, fears, stressors, etc. Consider again the curly part of the metal anchor that is twisted down into the ground. It is in the deep, cool earth. It is solid and unmovable. It gives you strength and a deeper point of reference. You are both the dog at the end of the cable and the metal tie out that anchors into the ground. When you are viewing life through the eyes of the dog, you are 100% at the *perspective of immersion.* When you are viewing life from the anchor point, and seeing the "dog" from a distance, you are 100% at the *perspective of elevation.* You can go back and forth as you choose or you can select anywhere along the length of the cable in between the two - partially immersed and partially elevated.

This visual metaphor helps me always remember that life is bigger than our daily grind and that we have a foundation of purpose, passion, love, and divinity that will always outlast any temporary storms or struggles. Through the proper lens, you can both achieve in the moment and also keep the bigger picture in mind!

As you paint your life's portrait,
consider perspective with each stroke.
What is the best zoom setting for you
to have at this moment? Think about a
time that you were most frustrated and
analyze your perspective in that moment.

Struggle

Through your experience in life to this point, you have experienced a lot. You have undoubtedly garnered wisdom. But what you have experienced so far and the knowledge you have gained is an appetizer with a full meal and dessert waiting for you just ahead.

Struggle comes in all sorts of forms. Heartbreak, sadness, fear, loss, anxiety, lack of confidence, "Imposter Syndrome", guilt, obsessiveness, loneliness, rejection, regret and the longing for something different or better than what is, are just a very few categoric examples.

One thing that I have learned to be true about life is that everyone is meant to find hardship and struggle. It is a natural part of life. It manifests differently for each one of us. For some people, struggle is obvious. For example, people have drug and alcohol addictions, have been confined to prison, lose their parents early in life, or are abused and abandoned. For these people, their struggles are easily visible to others. But for most people, struggle is less visible and can be judged as insignificant or less important... but they <u>are not</u> any less significant. What would seem like an insignificant nuisance to one person might be the hardship of a lifetime to someone else. The fact of the matter is that everyone's difficulties in life are just as important and significant as that of everyone else. The degree of someone's mental and emotional struggle is relative to that individual and not relative to other people. Never feel bad about feeling bad. You are allowed to have and express emotions. This is all part of being human.

Knowing and accepting that you will struggle through difficult times in life, in advance, will help you through whatever challenges you may face. Don't overreact. Knowing and accepting that it is not only *okay* to struggle, but it is actually good, expected, and beneficial in the long term is what I hope that you can fully embrace. Having life punch you in the face from time to time is a necessary and required part of the human experience.

Life is full of dichotomies. A dichotomy is when something is split into two mutually exclusive halves, often opposites. This concept is represented by the yin and yang symbol. Suffering through hard times in life is one half of one of these dichotomies. A person cannot truly appreciate life when all things are going well, unless they have also experienced life when it just sucks. For example, a child that is born a billionaire never appreciates his wealth nearly as much as the child born dirt poor that works hard to become a self-made billionaire.

Facing and triumphing through emotionally challenging times allows us to more fully experience joy and will bring the gift of gratitude to our hearts.

Sometimes you just have to *sit in the suck* and not run from it. I think of life as being full of alligator filled pits. It would make sense to walk around and avoid alligator-filled water if you could, right? But life doesn't work that way. There are no viable paths of avoidance. The only way is through the middle. To *sit in the suck* means to swim through the alligator pits, slowly and feeling the pain from each gator bite. Have you ever heard the saying: appreciate the good things in life? To *sit in the suck* means to appreciate the bad things in life. To learn and grow as a human, you can't avoid difficult situations. The only way to truly move yourself forward is going right through the middle of the alligator pits. As a side note, in the

1980's, a commonly used phrase to describe a bad situation was "the pits". People would say, "Oh, this is the pits." Maybe that should come back!

Struggles, challenges, and difficulties, internally and externally, will ebb and flow throughout your life. They will change in appearance, magnitude, and impact. Sometimes years will go by and you will wonder where all of your challenges have gone, then boom! An expected difficulty busts down your door. But, that's okay. Unknowingly, you will be ready for whatever challenges you face, and you will have the strength to endure because of all of which you have previously overcome. Each time you experience the worst of what life can offer you, the alligator pits, you are placing a new block into the foundation of your strength. It is this growth and reinforcement of your foundation that will build you into a stronger person and help carry you through anything that ever comes your way.

Olympian Will Faudree is a great example of resilience. As a talented young equestrian, he was thrown from his horse and sustained a life-threatening brain injury. After several months of intensive therapy, Will overcame this tremendous setback to become the United States Eventing Association's Rider of the Year. A few years later, in 2008, Will's sister, whom he was close to, was diagnosed with cancer and passed away shortly thereafter. In 2015, Will broke his neck after a fall from his horse.

Through all of this adversity Will Faudree has continued to endure and triumph to become an inspiration to other riders across his sport. Will has said, "Whenever things get hard or stressful, I always tell myself to keep going. We have no choice but to move forward, even if that means moving forward down a different path. You have to be honest with yourself about what you're facing and then make a plan. When things get hard, think in slow motion and figure out how to handle it. When I encounter obstacles, I keep going to the end."

Calm skies and smooth waters have never made a skilled sailor.

The necessity of learning to navigate rough waters in becoming a skilled sailor is the nexus between struggle and purpose. Believing that you will become a skilled sailor and accepting that storms are coming whether you like it or not will empower you and place you in a strong position to overcome even the strongest of storms. I will always be your biggest supporter and I am ever ready to pick you up when life knocks you down. When you were little and first learning to walk, you would fall often. But, I did not rush to pick you up and tell you everything was okay. I let you pick yourself up because I knew you could. If you couldn't, then I was always there for you. The same holds true to this day. I have total faith in your strength and resilience. Always know that I am here for you and whatever you need, but I ask you to pick yourself up, brush off the dirt and keep moving forward!

Have you already experienced
how some of the downturns
in your life have made
you more appreciative of
the joys in your life?

The One You Feed

There are two types of people in this world: victims and victors. Another way to phrase these two types of people is a quote from Henry Ford, who said, "There are two types of people in this world, those that think they can and those that think they can't … They are both right."

You actually get to choose which one you would like to be. Everyone gets to choose their own attitude. There are people with no material possessions that are thankful that they have everything they want in life. Also, there are people that own multiple homes, lavish cars, and inflated bank accounts that are upset every day because they believe that the world is set against them.

Mindset is an aggregate of thoughts and beliefs. Imagine that you are about to bake a cake for a special occasion. To bake anything from scratch, you always begin with individual ingredients: the flour, oil, eggs, etc., As baking relates to mindset, our thoughts represent the individual ingredients. We put all of our ingredients, i.e. thoughts, into the mixing bowl and then we blend them together with a spoon or mixer. Then we have our batter, which represents our beliefs. Our beliefs are an aggregate of our thoughts all mixed together. The new substance, the batter, is what we believe to be true.

How do we go from thoughts and beliefs to attitude and mindset? We put our batter in the oven and bake it. We end up with a cake and that represents our mindset about a particular slice of our life. Our mindset is the solidification of our beliefs. How does the cake taste? How does our attitude about a particular subject *feel*? Does your attitude feel like that of an inspired winner or one of a whiny victim? To understand the taste of your cake (the feel of your attitude) you only have to take an honest look at the ingredients. You are baking cakes all of the time without even knowing it.

Let's test your "ingredients" with the following questions about when you were in school:

How were your teachers in school? Did they pick on you? Did they not like you? Were they bad at what they did? Did they give you grades that were unfair?

…or…

Did you understand that you could have put forth a little more effort? Maybe you recognized that your teacher had a lot happening in their own lives and they were doing their best they could do? Perhaps you are thankful for when you asked your teacher for help and they tried their best to support you. Possibly you gave your teacher a gift or showed them a little kindness through a small gesture and the sentiment was returned in some way.

These are examples of two distinctly different "cakes". What were the ingredients of each?

Cake 1: Karen Cake

½ Cup of I Don't Feel Like Doing the Work

2 Teaspoons of I Should Get Without Having to Give

2 Cups of Life is Unfair

3 Ounces of It's Someone Else's Fault

Cake 2: Emily Cake

½ Cup of I am Capable of All Things

2 Teaspoons of Nothing Comes Easy So I Have to Work Hard

2 Cups of You Create "Luck" Through Preparation

3 Ounces of I am Thankful for Any Support That I Receive

When it comes to taste, the first cake might actually taste good. In fact, it can taste really good. But when you are finished eating it, you will have a stomach ache and will need to take a nap. But the taste of the second cake will also taste good but will also sustain you and empower you to overcome challenges, appreciate life, and achieve great things. Cake 1 is Victim and Cake 2 is Victor. It really is that simple. It all originates with your thoughts.

To maintain a positive and productive mindset, be a conscientious gatekeeper of your thoughts.

To properly evaluate the quality of your thoughts, send them through some litmus tests. For example, are your thoughts from a perspective of immersion or of elevation? Are your thoughts aligning with your life's purposes? Are your own thoughts inspiring to you? Are you proud of these thoughts? Would you share your thoughts with your Mom?

A great book on this subject is a quick little read titled "As a Man Thinketh" by James Allen. The author grew up poor in England in the 1800's. Allen described his book in this way:

"I have tried to make the book simple, so that all can easily grasp and follow its teaching, and put into practice the methods which it advises. It shows how, in his own thought-world, each man holds the key to every condition, good or bad, that enters into his life, and that, by working patiently and intelligently upon his thoughts, he may remake his life, and transform his circumstances."

Allen understood that the base ingredients of life's circumstances are your thoughts. They are controllable, changeable, and powerful. Thoughts literally build your life. They create reality as you see and experience it. Thoughts possess powerful energy that determine how life unfolds for you. Always test them to make sure they will serve you. Ensure that your thoughts will mobilize you to achieve your goals. Consciously consider if they are the right thoughts that will help build you into the person that you want to be and build the life that you want for yourself.

The question of victim or victor is only answered from within.

There is a commonly known parable that further emphasizes the power of our thoughts. It is the story of two wolves.

There was an old Cherokee chief that explained to his grandson, a little boy, that there are two hungry wolves living inside each of us. These wolves are always fighting one another. The first wolf is very hungry. He was described by the Chief as one of small, self-serving thoughts. This wolf is consumed with getting as much as he can at the expense of others. This wolf is greedy and unkind. He views himself as a victim and tells lies to himself and others. He masquerades his fears and feelings of inferiority with a thin exterior of false toughness and foul arrogance. There is an ugliness to his thoughts and a coldness within his heart. The second wolf is also very hungry. But he will share the meal with his pack, perhaps eating last. He prioritizes kindness above shallow gratification. He is at peace with himself and with life. He possesses much wisdom and understands that darkness cannot exist in the presence of light - That love always conquers all. This wolf sees the beauty in all things.

The little boy, frightened at the prospect of being overtaken by Wolf #1 asked, "Which wolf will win?"

The Chief answered, "The one you feed."

Which one will win? The one you feed.

I have the utmost faith in you to never make yourself into a victim of life's circumstances, but instead to carry a mindset laced with resilience and gratitude, kindness and servitude. I encourage you to use your thoughts to help propel you forward. Think big. Imagination is a form of thought, too. All things in life, all inventions, all accomplishments, all achievements were first only thoughts. If you can imagine it, you can achieve it!

As you are creating each
day for yourself, how are
your thoughts coloring and
affecting your experiences?

Failure

Failure is often a specific source of struggle as talked about in Cheat Code 4. The most successful head coach in the history of the National Football League is Bill Belichick. The New England Patriots, with Belichick as their head coach have played in nine Superbowls and won six. The second most Superbowls won by any other head coach is four. Everyone pictures Bill on the sideline of a football field in his infamous New England Patriots hooded sweatshirt. But what people either don't know or easily forget is that Bill wasn't always the head coach of the Patriots. His head coaching career began with the Cleveland Browns, where over five years he lost more games than he won. In only one of his five seasons did his team have a winning record.

So, with the Cleveland Browns only 20% of his seasons were "winning". Belichick was fired. Subsequently, he was selected as the interim head coach for the New York Jets, but he was not selected for the permanent position, being overlooked for someone else. Then, finally, after twenty-five years of holding various coaching jobs in the NFL, and after his failed head coaching experience in Cleveland, Coach Belichick was selected to be the head coach for New England. In twenty-four seasons, Bill has led the Patriots to twenty winning seasons, or an 83% success. Was Coach Belichick a failure during his five years in Cleveland? No, he was successfully learning how to be better.

"You are a failure..." That is a powerful statement. But, if someone told me that I was a failure, I would respond by saying, "thank you!"

There are many great quotes about failure. Here are a few of my favorites:

Winston Churchill: "Success is stumbling from failure to failure with no loss of enthusiasm."

Thomas Edison: "I have not failed. I've just found 10,000 ways that won't work."

Robert Kennedy: "Only those who dare to fail greatly can ever achieve greatly."

When you think of yourself as a failure, be proud.

Your failures are more valuable and informative than your successes. Life is like a scavenger hunt. There is a clue waiting for you each time you fail at something. Each clue gives you information about how to find success in what you are seeking. Then you fail again, and you are given another clue. Then you fail again, but you are given another clue.

Some scavenger hunts may take you only one clue, for you to find the pathway to success. But many others may take numerous clues and many years to complete. Unfortunately, some people never solve their own scavenger puzzles. This is because they don't understand the value of their own failures. So many people don't understand that hidden within each failure is important experience and critical information. Instead, they can't get past their emotional responses to failure, and label themselves in negative ways. A lack of resilience wins out and they tell themselves lies about their lack of abilities and potential. They underestimate themselves and assign credibility to their harshest critics.

If you don't understand the value of failure, then you will miss the clue. If you aren't seeking the coded information hidden under the rock because you are too busy whining and feeling sorry for yourself, then how could you ever complete the scavenger hunt? Success in anything worthwhile can *only* be found through failure. The path to success is certainly paved by the bricks of failure. But keeping your head up and chest out takes a lot of internal strength. You must commit to not being deterred. Your will to prevail must be strong. Just like Will Faudree, just keep going.

Just keep going!

Believe in yourself and envision eventual success. But most importantly, never forget for a moment that I believe in you 100%, and will always be proud of your failures, too!

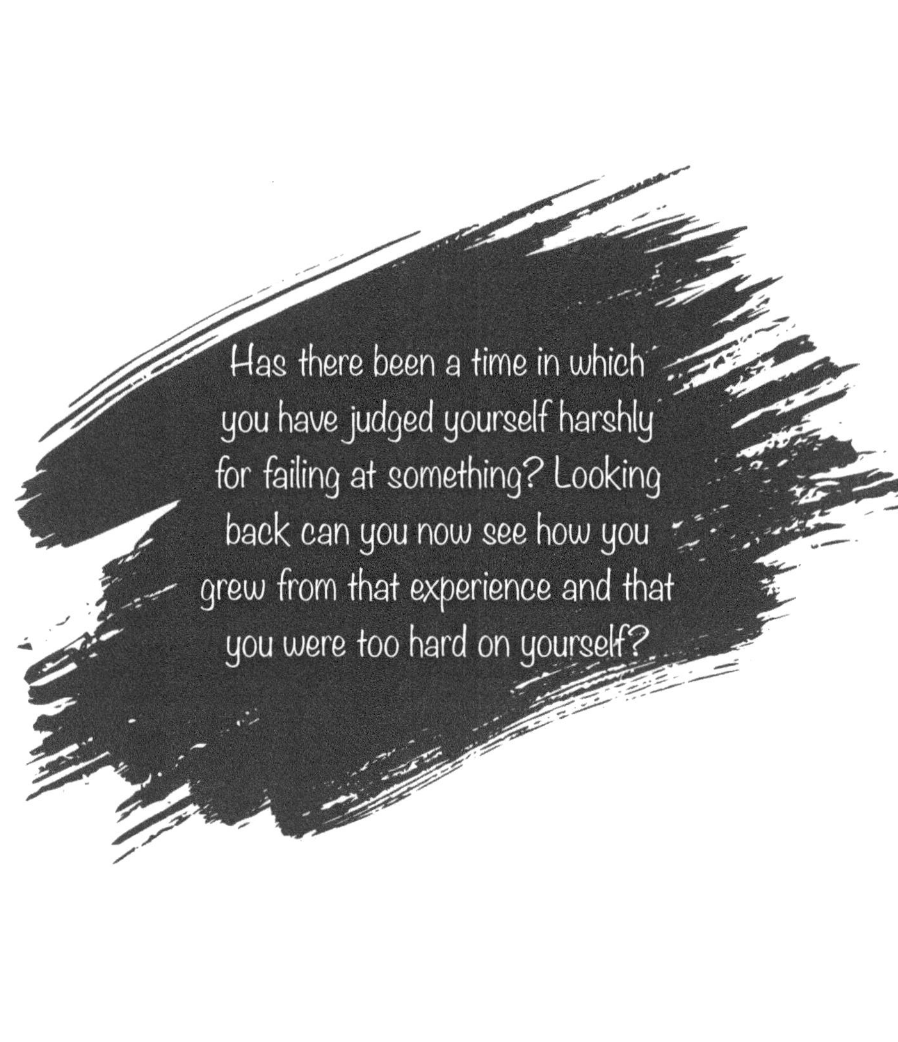

Has there been a time in which
you have judged yourself harshly
for failing at something? Looking
back can you now see how you
grew from that experience and that
you were too hard on yourself?

Push Yourself

The truth is that most people are too afraid to fail and therefore never dip their toe into the water of personal, emotional discomfort. To achieve anything great, you have to start getting comfortable with the uncomfortable.

One of my favorite quotes is from the author Iyanla Vanzant who said,

"If there's not something in your life that pushes you to

the point where the pee is running down your leg, then you ain't living big enough".

Personal growth only occurs when you intentionally get out of your comfort zone. Fortunately, though, like anything else, the more you practice at getting uncomfortable, the better you get at being uncomfortable.

There was a point in my life that it occurred to me that I wanted to be a leader in my organization and in my profession. So, I committed to making some positive changes in my daily habits by reading more and spending less time wasting away in front of a television screen. I enrolled in college to obtain a graduate degree. I was all-in. What I realized, though, was that all leaders have the ability to speak in front of groups of people; I did not. Like so many people, when speaking in front of others, I would be overcome with the fight or flight symptoms of performance anxiety. My hands sweated, my voice cracked and became shaky. I would be so embarrassed that I would cut short whatever I was trying to say just so I could end my presentation as quickly as possible and get back to a comfortable place. I was faced with a challenge; one that seemed as dangerous as a pit of alligators.

Deep down, I knew there was no way around this treacherous pit. The only way to get to the other side was to go right through the middle. I found, deep within myself, the will and determination to do exactly that. I confided in my wife that I was having terrible trouble with public speaking. I told her how I wanted to conquer this fear and overcome this barrier to becoming a strong leader. As luck, or divinity, would have it, she mentioned that she saw an advertisement in the local newspaper about a local Toastmasters club that was just forming and looking for members.

"What the hell is Toastmasters?" I asked.

I pictured a culinary group that worked on perfecting how to brown a piece of bread. I was intrigued to find out that Toastmasters has nothing to do with food, but is instead an international non-profit organization that is dedicated to helping people become great public speakers, and great leaders. Sometimes the universe (or God) gives you just what you need, when you need it.

I went to this local club's initial meeting and before I knew it, I was vice president of this tiny, local Toastmasters club. We practiced speeches and worked hard to grow the group. We recruited other people from the community and found that the fear of public speaking is ubiquitous in our society. A diverse group of people, of all ages and backgrounds, came from miles around to join our group. A few years later, when our family moved to a new home is when I stepped away from our group. I had helped build a strong club of people helping others through mutual support and encouragement. After years of practice, I was starting to gain a fair amount of confidence and competence in my own public speaking ability.

Toastmasters was just what I needed. But, it was only half of the equation for me. The other half had to come from the inside.

As a kid, one of my favorite movies was "Where the Red Fern Grows", which was based on the book by Wilson Rawls. In this story, a young boy named Billy has a burning desire to purchase his very own coon hunting dogs. The boy's family was very poor and good hunting dogs were very expensive. So, he discussed his wish with his wise grandfather. Billy told his grandpa that he thought that God doesn't want him to have any hunting dogs. He explained that he has asked God for dogs for as long as he can remember, but nothing had yet happened. The grandfather told Billy that if he wanted dogs bad enough, he will get them. But if he wanted God's help, then he would have to meet God halfway. In other words, you have to do your part. You have to commit your will and be ready to do whatever it takes.

I had the will to succeed and to become a strong leader. To achieve the things in life that I wanted to achieve, I knew that I had to become a proficient public speaker. I committed to myself. I promised myself. I decided to meet God halfway and felt that God had already done His part. The fear of failure would not defeat me. I decided to never, ever decline an opportunity to speak in public. Strategically, I knew that the more I practiced the better I would get. Why would I ever turn down an opportunity to practice? The only answer I could come up with was fear - the fear of failure. In the 17 years since I made this commitment to myself, I have never turned down an opportunity to speak.

Many, many times I have failed. I have embarrassed myself. I have heard people make fun of me. At times it was hard, but, I kept my head up and chest out. I forced myself to be proud of myself. Who else has the courage to propel themselves out of their comfort zone so far and so often? I absolutely knew I was going to fail, but I accepted it on the front side. I envisioned success. I prepared. I did the best I could. But sometimes, it just didn't go well. Maybe I didn't properly gauge my audience; maybe I tried to make a joke that didn't land; maybe my old ways came about and I just got overly nervous. But I was okay with it. I knew I was just walking down the path to success, on the firm bricks of failure.

Now I am generally comfortable talking in front of hundreds of people. But my comfort zone still has boundaries. Just last year I was asked to deliver an opening prayer to a meeting of about eighty people. I have spoken to an audience that size many times, but I had never *prayed* with an audience. I didn't want to do it…at all. Public prayer is not my cup of tea. I remembered my commitment and knew that my reluctance was informing me that I needed to do it. The pact with myself does not expire. My commitment to self-growth isn't over. So I did it. It was so-so, at best. I'm proud of my courage and I will do it again if the opportunity arises. Since I made that original promise to myself, I have become viewed by many people, including myself, as a leader and strong public speaker. I have been promoted at work three times and have found the success in life that I was seeking. I hope my example of how I got comfortable with discomfort will inspire you to punch fear right in its face.

> # Fear is just another bully that backs down when courageously confronted.

I want to underscore the importance and power of true will. To push yourself out of your comfort zone, it takes a lot of courage, but it also takes the will to commit to something hard and to keep going when it gets even harder. If you want to achieve hard things, great things, then it will take the will to do whatever is necessary. Another way to think of the word will is determination. Will is like a superhero suit that you put on your body before jumping into the alligator pits that we have previously discussed.

Strong will and determination make you jump in the water, then helps you float, propels you through the water, and keeps the gator bites from hurting as much. Without will and determination, you may never jump into the pit, and if you do, you won't swim very far. So, I encourage you to put your suit on with will and determination in all that you do, then jump in with both feet and don't look back!

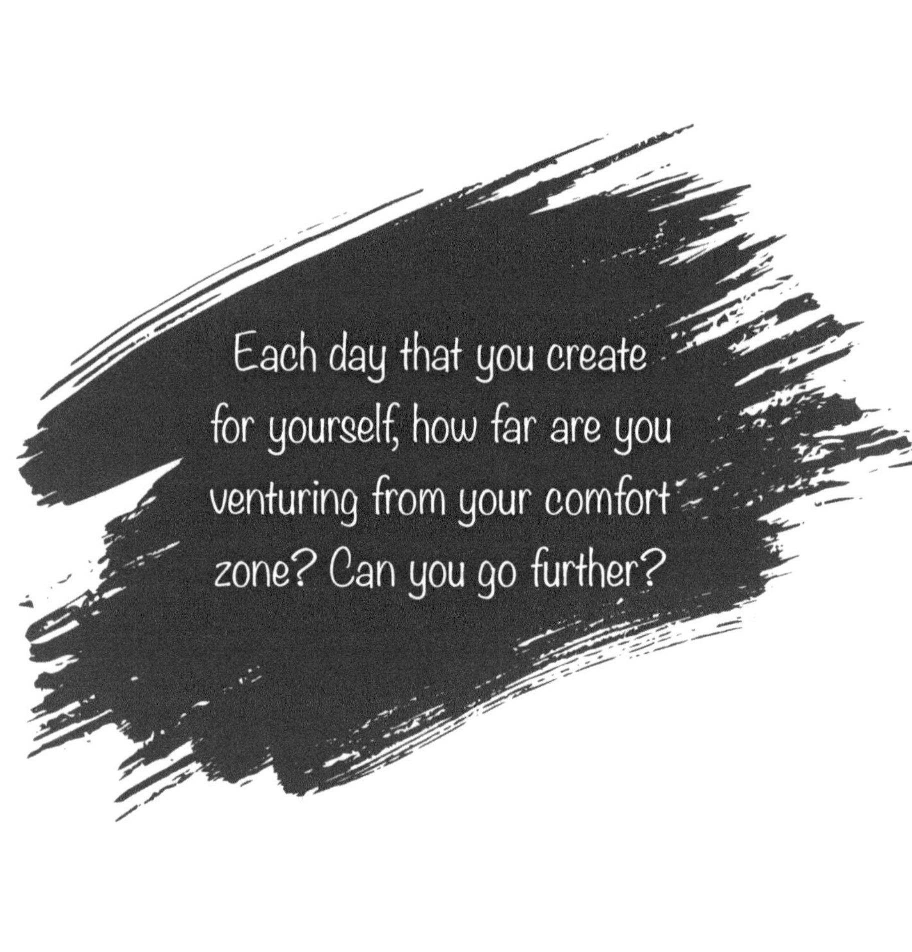

Each day that you create
for yourself, how far are you
venturing from your comfort
zone? Can you go further?

Connection

As of 2023, there are over 8 billion people living on Earth. This makes the human being as the most common creature that we will encounter every day of our lives. Unless we want to move to an isolated part of the world or become an angry hermit, we will see and interact with multiple people every day for the rest of our lives.

People will come and go, in and out of your life, at

the right time, for the right reasons.

How we view and interact with people has a tremendous effect on our lives. I can't help but think of our basset hound, Teddy-bear. He likes to venture on public hiking trails with us, but he gets extremely scared every time a fellow hiker crosses his path. He lurches downward, his tail goes up and curls over his back, and he barks with suspicion. Teddy-bear views human beings as frightening. What Teddy-bear doesn't know is that from this world and the people in it, you get back what you put out. An old African proverb informs us that if you want to go fast go alone, if you want to go far go together.

If you want to go fast go alone, if you want to go far go together.

Through human connection, we are given the power to move mountains within ourselves. From other people, we can draw immense inspiration to shoot for the stars and at the same time know that we have protection and support in case we fall. Human connection is the key that unlocks so many doors that lay in front of you. World class equestrian Will Faudree described his illustrious career by saying, "I don't have a ton of wins that stand out. It's more about the relationships and friendships I've made. Seeing the joy, excitement, and passion in others inspires me."

Have you ever received a random message or gift from a friend or acquaintance that just brightened your day? If so, then somebody chose to give you a little love and inspiration that day.

One of my favorite early morning activities is logging on to Facebook and sending random messages to friends, acquaintances and sometimes people I barely know. I always send some variation of the same message: "Good morning John. Have a great day today". I don't worry about how the message will be received. I don't worry about the person's reaction to it. I don't care at all if they don't respond. It's an easy exercise in choosing to spread love and just having faith in the result.

Reactions to receiving little messages of happiness and encouragement are almost always positive. Sometimes people are a little freaked out. At times people don't respond at all. I don't care about those non-positive responses because before I even send the message, I have let go of any attachment to the result. I don't hold it against them. I couldn't even tell you who I've sent messages to that haven't responded. Really, I couldn't care less and it's a wonderful and peaceful feeling to be relieved of the expectation of a certain reciprocation or outcome.

On the flip side, I can't tell you how awesomely often I have received this particular response to my morning message, "OMG. You don't know how much I needed that right now. Thank you so much!"

My impactful Facebook exercise is a metaphor for life. Everybody needs to receive a little love from others, even from people they may barely know or not know at all. When a kind and loving message is unexpected and timely it can be crazy powerful. You can be uncommonly kind and not worry about what happens after. It will be okay. Nobody is offended by kindness. The best part is that the warm feeling that you give others from your kindness almost immediately manifests inside of yourself, too.

What you put out in this world is what you get back. Do you want people to like you? Then like people. Do you want people to be kind? Then be kind. Do you want people to not judge you? Then don't judge people. Do you want people to not speak poorly of you? Right, then don't.

All decisions, literally ALL decisions, that are made in life are the result of human relationships. Stop and think about this. Test it.

<u>All</u> decisions are the result of human relationships.

Just like the fear of public speaking, many people possess the fear of human connection and intimacy. Boiled down to their origin, these fears are cascaded from the fear of being judged. If you keep drilling down, you finally get back to the fear of failure. Consider what we have already discussed about the fear of failure. Might you develop a relationship with someone that eventually rejects you? That judges you? That ostracizes you? That hurts you? Of course!

These failures are just failures of a different color. Everyone knows the old saying that it is better to have loved and lost than to never have loved at all. I encourage you to be bold in connecting with others. Say the hard thing, such as "I appreciate you" or "I love you".

Be boldly kind.

The truth is that what you put out in this world is what you get back. People will mirror you. For example, when you don't look people in the eyes, people won't connect with you. When you don't smile at people, nobody will smile at you. But the opposite is also true! Kindness brings kindness.

You get what you do.

Imagine a bathroom faucet. Picture the end of the spout where the water comes out. If you unscrew the end of it, there is a little screen that filters the water. If you ever look at this filter you will see all of the hard water calcification that has built up from daily use. It is full of chalk that blocks the flow of the water. After someone cleans that little screen, water flows from the faucet easily and freely. Our hearts are very much the same. We all have hardness around our soft centers. But, just like the calcification in our faucets and shower heads, we can clean the outer edges of our hearts. We can knock that hardness off and, just like the water coming out of our faucet, our life will begin to flow more smoothly and clearly with less of a broken stream.

Navigating through life's myriad of diverse personalities can be quite challenging. Some people are just difficult to be around. There are strategies to overcome some of these difficulties. Think about a relationship that causes you strife. Maybe someone at school or work that seems to always be working against you or maybe someone in your family that always finds a way to blame you for their problems. Consider how thoughts about and interactions with this person make you feel inside. Your blood pressure rises, your heart rate increases; maybe you feel anxiety or queasiness when you imagine speaking to this person.

One tactic that I employ is to remember that we are literally all from the same place and the same source. Consider that the other person probably isn't *trying* to be a problem for you. Go a step further and ask yourself, "what is the most loving thought that I can have in this situation?" Before you try answering that question, dig deep into your soul and answer these questions:

Do you believe that you should judge other people? Of course not, then stop.

Do you believe that your judgments of other people should be the determining factor of their worth? Of course not, everyone has tremendous worth.

Do you think this person should be denied kindness in their life because of how you perceive or judge them? The truth is that the people that trouble us the most are actually most in need of a little additional kindness and support. This truth was emphasized over 2400 years ago by the great thinker and philosopher Plato who said, "Be kind for everyone you meet is fighting a hard battle." In more recent times, Author Brad Meltzer is credited with saying it differently with, "Everyone is fighting a battle you know nothing about."

Everyone is fighting a battle you know nothing about.

When people say derogatory things about other people, it is always a reflection about how they feel deep down about themselves. It is projection. Harsh words and character assassinations are swords and shields that are used to try to hide feelings of low self-worth, incompetence, and insecurity. People that constantly attack other people are actually those among us that need kindness the most because they are frequently hurting on the inside.

Now back to the question: What is the most loving thought you can have about someone that causes you unease? The answer is probably something like "This person needs and deserves love." Maybe it is "It wouldn't kill me to be kind to them; they probably really need it."

Now you ask yourself: What is the most loving thing you can say to this person? If you are focused on your judgments of this person, then this question is very difficult to answer. Maybe the most loving thing that you can do, then, next time you encounter your trouble-person is acknowledging their existence alongside yours with just one simple, loving, beautiful word. "Hi.".

If you release your judgments of other people, especially those people that trouble you most, then you can slowly start to remove the calcification around your heart, which is inside of everyone. You can make the conscious choice to begin with a screwdriver and hammer and to start chipping away at any hardness that you have been building and have allowed others to place upon your heart.

The end result is living in a state of natural flow. Like the water in a clean faucet, life and love will more easily flow through you and what comes out of you will be purer; more truly you. Eventually, you will view humans as what they actually are: vulnerable, yet powerful connectors to something bigger than ourselves.

In the end, at our funeral, we only leave one thing behind; just one thing. It's the impact that we've had on the people that we've encountered throughout our life.

In the end, the only thing we leave behind is the impact that we've had on the people that we've encountered throughout our life.

I think about this very thing at every funeral I attend. People don't stand around and talk about how much money someone has earned, about the size of their house, or their popularity. When it is my time to go, I know that people will discuss what impact I may have had on them. Recounting funny stories or maybe remembering something I said to them or experienced with them. These are the good things in life; simple things. Perhaps seeming trivial in the moment, but sometimes a little bit of kindness is remembered for the rest of someone's life. I encourage you to embrace the vulnerability of laying down your personal barriers to truly connect with others. I have total faith in you to prioritize kindness in and to make strong and meaningful relationships with the deserving people in your life!

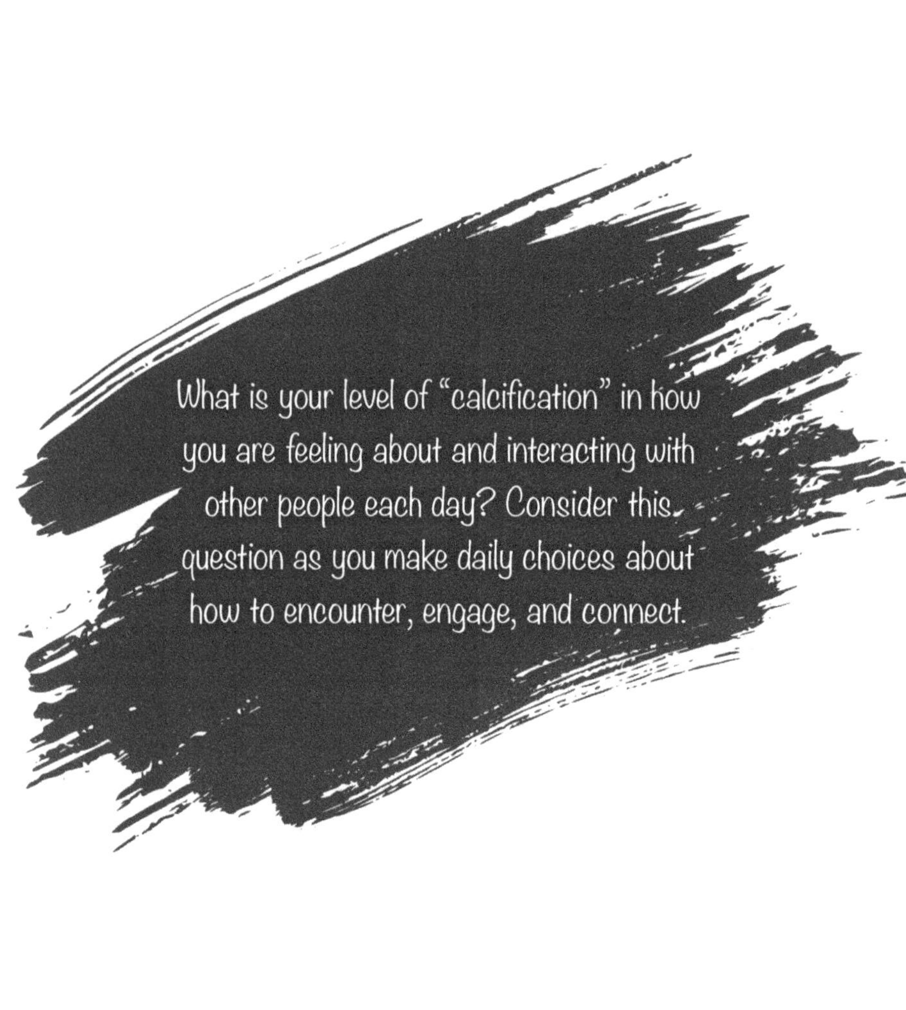

What is your level of "calcification" in how
you are feeling about and interacting with
other people each day? Consider this
question as you make daily choices about
how to encounter, engage, and connect.

Meaning

Everyone should read the book *Man's Search for Meaning* by Victor Frankl. A psychiatrist prior to and after WWII, Dr. Frankl lived through the worst possible human conditions as a prisoner of Auschwitz and Dachau. Dr. Frankl tells us that people can withstand and overcome any set of circumstances if they understand their reason for living, their purpose, their "why". Dr. Frankl stated, "Those who have a 'why' to live can bear with almost any 'how'".

"Those who have a 'why' to live can bear with almost any 'how'".

At a certain point in my journey, I introspectively examined the purpose of my life. I didn't just question the meaning of life in general terms, but specifically, unique to me, I asked, "What is my life's purpose? Why was I born? What are the types of things that I am supposed to be doing while here on Earth? What are the thoughts and behaviors that float up from my deepest, yet richest wells of my existence?"

I will share with you my deeply personal findings so that you can have an authentic example of how these questions can be answered.

Through authentic self-examination I determined that I have six life purposes:

1. Give Unconditional Love

I try to live my life with this as a primary foundation. I choose to view people as divine beings that are all deserving of my love and kindness. I wish not to and try not to judge the core of another person as anything less. I may dislike what they say, do, and display on the surface, but I recognize them as something greater than that. I certainly fail at this high purpose on some days, but I do my best.

2. Show Empathy

I have always had a strong ability to put myself in someone else's shoes. I can understand both sides of a disagreement or conflict. Empathy is a powerful way to let someone know that they are not alone and that someone else can understand their plight.

3. Inspire and Encourage Others

I recognize this as a skill or ability that has been granted to me. Innately, I want to coach people to be better versions of themselves.

4. Lift People Up

This is similar but different from #3. When people are feeling sad, depressed, mournful, or discouraged, I feel the strong need to help. A small act of kindness can help get somebody back on track or find a little peace in a tough situation.

5. Teach

I feel this desire and ability within my inner being. Teaching is a means of inspiring and encouraging others, which furthers my ability to achieve purpose #3. I believe it is much more admirable to share than it is to know!

6. Learn

How could I ever empathize with others, inspire, encourage, lift, or teach others if I am not excited about learning from others and from life itself?

Those are _my_ six life purposes. They are unique to me and my life. Contemplation of these purposes help ground and guide me through life's various episodes. They give me strength and minimize fear. No matter what could ever happen in my life, these things could never be taken away from me. Think about it from an occupational standpoint. Even if I got fired from my job today, my life's purpose would not be lost. I can live these purposes in almost any occupation that I choose. Could I give love as a grocery store clerk? Could I show empathy as a school janitor? Could I encourage and lift people as an Uber driver? Of course, I could!

Your life's purposes are a large part of the dog tie-out concept that we discussed in Cheat Code 3. They help make up the terra that anchors the metal tie-out. Identifying and understanding *your* life's purposes and meaning and living with them within arm's reach, for when you need to remember and review, is one of the most important secrets of life that I can share with you. When you are the dog, barking at the delivery driver, and you're not sure which way to go next, just trace yourself back to your anchor point and you will feel the strength of your foundation...your purpose, passion, values, family, and home.

Author Dr. Wayne Dyer told us, "Don't die with your music still in you." By the word music, Dr. Dyer was referring to our purpose and meaning. These should be our ultimate guides and we must not be afraid to live out our purpose.

Let your "music"
unabashedly be heard by all.

At this point in your life, understanding your life's purpose may not be as easy as it is for an old geezer like me. Perhaps, you may only be able to identify one or two life's purposes and those may change over time, and that's great. If you are giving a little thought and consideration to purpose and meaning, you will be ahead of the game. I know your life has an important purpose. You will find and understand this purpose more clearly as you progress through each stage of life in your future. Don't fret about it, but don't forget about it. I have faith in you to find your meaning in life and to live that purpose to the fullest!

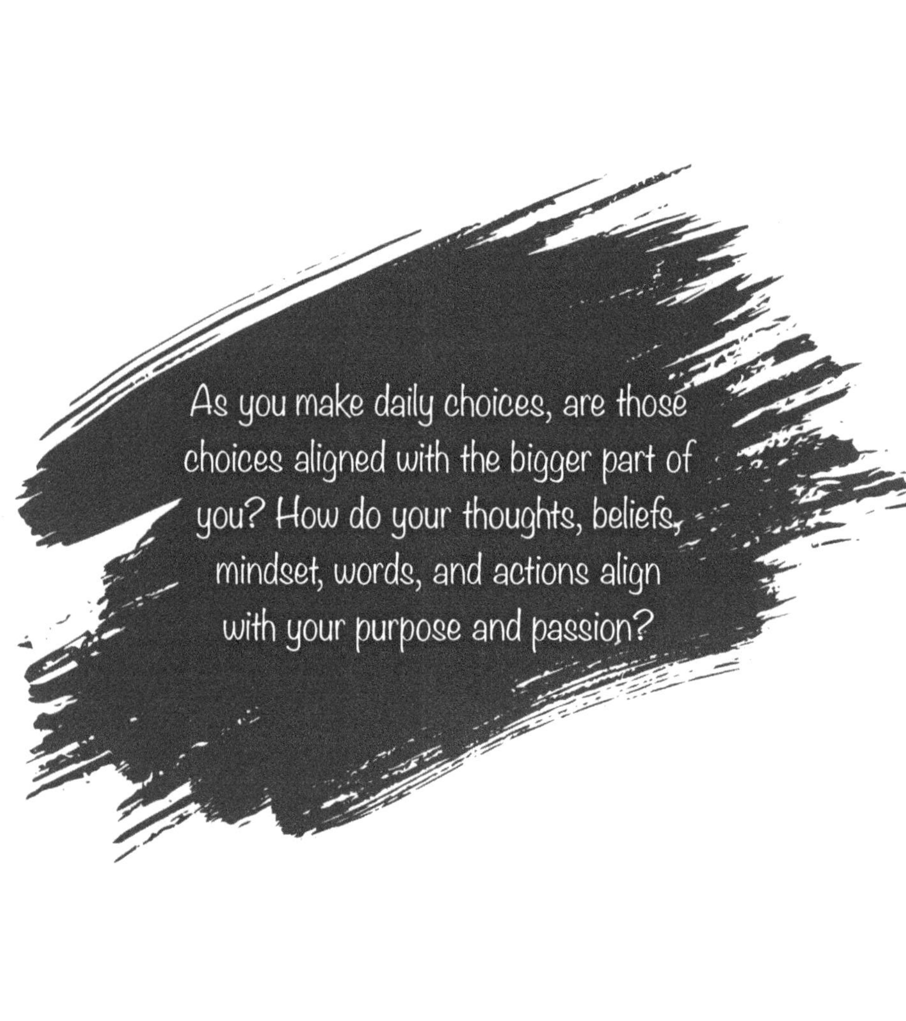
As you make daily choices, are those choices aligned with the bigger part of you? How do your thoughts, beliefs, mindset, words, and actions align with your purpose and passion?

Be Quiet and Listen

As much as I would love to follow you around every day and give you advice about what to do, how to do things, what to say, or not say, where to go, and how to live…I don't think you want or need that! There is another, more practicable resource to help guide you in life. This resource is available to you 24 hours a day, 7 days a week. No, good guess, but it's not Google. I'm talking about the little, quiet voice that exists within; your internal wisdom. Whether someone believes that this wisdom originates from Jesus, God, your higher self, a dead relative, your subconscious, or something else, that doesn't matter. You can believe your little voice is created by whomever or whatever you want. What is important for you to know is that your little voice is _always_ there for you, if you choose to seek it out and listen to it. Another word for this little voice is intuition.

Seek out your little, quiet voice and follow it.

To be able to properly hear your little voice, you have to get yourself and your mind quiet. For many people the perfect time for this is immediately after prayer. Whereas prayer is talking to God, I am telling you to _listen_ to God. This is sometimes referred to as meditation. I'm not asking you to sit in a cave in the mountains of Tibet or under a tree overlooking the ocean. I'm not suggesting that you sit cross-legged with your thumb and forefinger in a circle while humming. What I am telling you is to sit quietly and listen.

The trick is that you have to quiet your regular thoughts. Imagine a buried treasure. You have to remove the dirt with a shovel to expose the gold that lies beneath. Finding your little, quiet voice inside of you is much like uncovering a buried treasure, as you have to sift through and shovel away all of your useless mental chatter.

To accomplish this, start by simply being quiet and sitting in a quiet space for 5 minutes or longer. Your mind will want to race away with random thoughts and that's okay. You can counteract your mental chatter by focusing on something else, such as your breathing. For example, feel the air you breathe gently moving across the skin on the inside of your nose. Feel the sensation of your chest rhythmically rising with each inhalation and do the same as the air is gently escaping you. At the very beginning, start out by doing this for even just one minute. Paying attention to your breath for only sixty seconds is wonderfully refreshing. You likely won't hear your inner voice in just one minute, but nonetheless, this short and simple exercise can provide a marvelous mental and emotional decluttering. If you progress this exercise to five or ten minutes, or longer, and make it part of your daily habits, you will find the true gold. Anxiety lessens. Thoughts become clearer.

Can you recall that great feeling that you get when you have a clean room or clean house, with a fresh scent, or perhaps the fabulous feeling of fresh and clean bedsheets? That is how your life starts to feel if you just get quiet and listen every day.

Once your mind is quiet, the stage is set for your little, quiet voice to whisper. That little voice will sound like your regular inner-thoughts, but it will be subtly different. Your little voice may not be a voice at all. It may be just a feeling or a mental image. When it is just a feeling, people refer to it as your "gut" or "gut feeling". No matter the means of perception, the point is that we can find much wisdom and guidance from within ourselves if we do the things necessary to discover it.

We can find wisdom and guidance from within ourselves if we do the things necessary to discover it.

If on any given day, you are struggling with direction, before you begin to quiet your thoughts, ask yourself a question for which you are seeking the answer. Such as, how do I handle this situation? What should I do about this? Then quiet your mind for five or ten minutes and see what happens. Even if you don't hear anything, you are participating in a very worthwhile exercise because, at a minimum, you are grounding yourself. Sometimes your answers come at that time, and sometimes your answers will come a little later. But if you are paying attention, answers will usually come.

On the rare occasion in my life that I had a fairly big decision to make, I have followed the advice that I had read in a book, *Frequency* by Penney Peirce, years ago.

Here's what you do to help make a big decision. Sit or lie down in a quiet space. But if you lie down, make sure you are not sleepy. Get your mind quiet of your mental chatter and focus on the question at hand. After a few minutes, think about one of the options you are considering. Imagine that you actually already chose that option. Don't consider all of the various intricacies that accompany that choice, just imagine that you selected that particular option. Next, take inventory of how you feel. Do you feel excited? Energized? Motivated? Joyous? Peaceful? Warm? How does your body feel? Does this decision literally give you good feelings throughout your body? Or are you feeling heavy, worried, sad, or uncomfortable? After considering option one for this big decision, move to option two and go through the same process, then to option three, etc. Which one of the decision options made you *feel* the best? This is an example of how your intuition can help guide you to where you need to go, if you seek it out and listen to it.

There are a million books, online videos, and other resources about how to meditate and how to connect with your intuition. I have really just provided you with the tip of the iceberg and what works for me. It is up to you to further learn about these things, if you so choose. I have found my little voice inside of me to be very helpful throughout my life. I encourage you to not discount your own inner wisdom, but instead to discover and trust it!

Have you ever heard or felt your little, quiet voice? Try to think of a time in your life that you didn't follow your "gut" and regretted it.

The Workforce.

A Word is Dead
When it is Said,
Some Say.
I Say it Just
It Just
Begins to Live
That Day.
~Emily Dickinson

There is a scene in the original Superman movie that shows young Clark Kent leaving his adopted parents and their Kansas home. But before he goes, he is instinctively led to walk out to a shed to discover the glowing crystal that contains immeasurable power. When I consider the power of words, I think of that crystal.

Words are the representatives of your thoughts.

Your words are your personal workforce. They do the heavy lifting and carrying of taking what is inside of you to the outside. They distribute your thoughts, opinions, attitudes, desires, and hopes and display them for the world to see. The greater vocabulary that you have, the more workers you employ. You are the boss. Your workers, i.e. your words, are very obedient and are directed by you alone.

If you tell your workers not to take the actual goods from your inside, but to take imposter goods instead, then they will. Your words are capable of showing false inventory. This creates what is known as cognitive dissonance. This is the hallmark of inauthenticity.

If you tell your workers to carry out only the minimum amount of product to stay in compliance with society, then they will leave most of the treasures on the inside. This is the hallmark of shyness.

If you tell your workers to select and display the goods that appear to make you look and sound better than other people, then they will. This is the hallmark of an inferiority complex.

If you tell your workers to select only the hurtful goods, oh they will. The goods they bring out will function as knives and swords; thus, you will be perceived as hurtful and unkind.

These examples could go on and on, but the point is that you are the CEO of this very loyal and subservient workforce. How you develop and direct your workforce will influence every aspect of your life. Your words can draw people to you or push them away. Your words can inspire or disgust. The direction you give to them will be a large determinant in the success of your life and the amount and sustainability of your happiness.

Above all else, I hope that *my* words are purveyors of love. That is the direction that I give to my workforce, as guided by my life purposes. I envision taking my words from my throat and dipping them down into my heart before they exit my mouth. I imagine that when they dip into my heart that they come out with a coating, like chocolate dipped pretzels. The visual of love-dipped words help me, not only in choosing specific words, but also in choosing how, when, and why to speak.

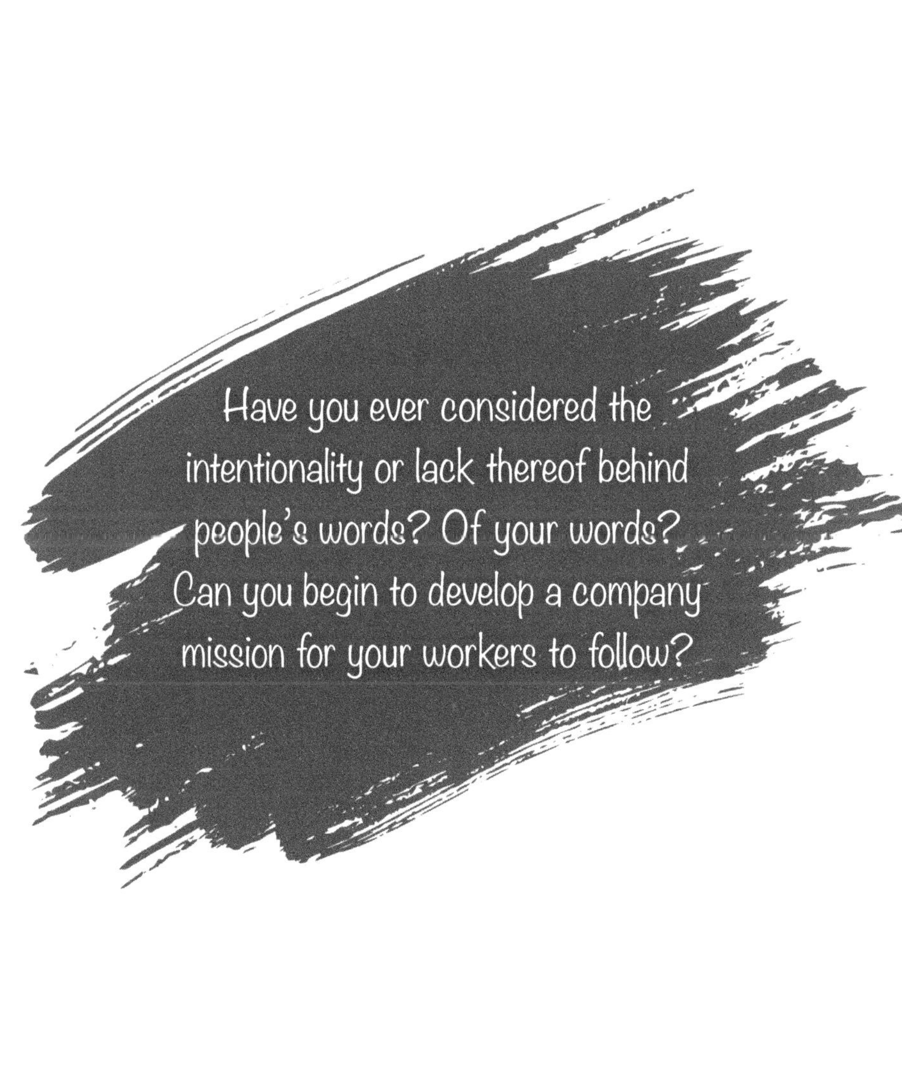
Have you ever considered the intentionality or lack thereof behind people's words? Of your words? Can you begin to develop a company mission for your workers to follow?

Love

If you believe that you live in an unloving world, then you will live in an unloving world. If you think that the world is devoid of love then you will never experience it. In contrast, if you believe that love is ubiquitously all around you, then you can literally feel it within every breath and every rise and fall of your chest. You will see love in people that do not see it in themselves.

Love is what binds us together as people. If you are willing to remove the barriers that hide it, then you can expose it to be everywhere that you are. It exists with you in every moment. I know this because my love for you is never paused and never ending. But, that's just one source for you. There are many more. You get what you give.

Be a loving person and you will be filled up in return.

It's the most basic of our instincts. It's the reason for our existence. It feeds and warms our souls. When you consciously and intentionally choose thoughts, words, and actions that are loving to other people, then you can let go of any worry that you may have about the outcome related to your choice. When you choose love at the outset, then you can have faith in how things will turn out. What bad outcome can come from love? A broken heart will be mended and is better than no heart at all.

Choosing love in your words
and actions will lead to a
more peaceful and productive
life, one with more fulfilling
relationships and a clearer
purpose.

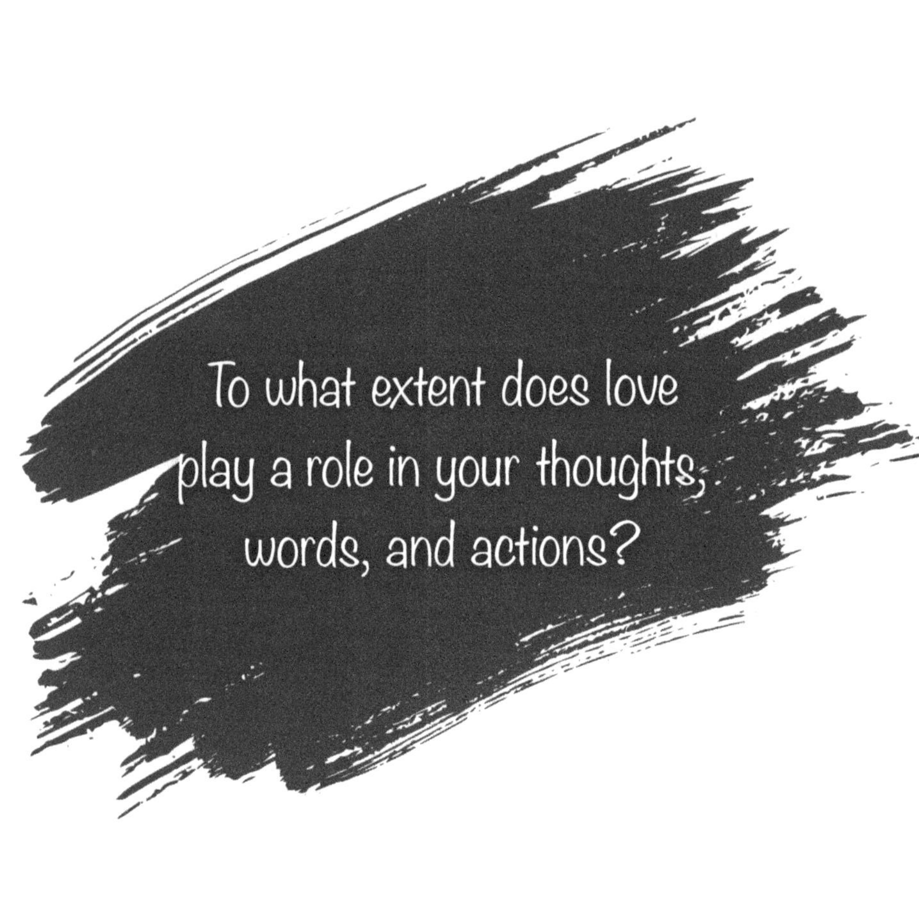
To what extent does love
play a role in your thoughts,
words, and actions?

Conclusion

It takes courage to bust away from the shelters and supports of the place and people that you call home. Please know that your home is a place that is always awaiting your return. The family members that dwell there will be saddened by your absence, but excited for you to embark upon this new and exciting journey. We are very proud of you and love you immeasurably. As you set sail, please remember the wisdom given to you herein.

Life is short so make the most of it.
Be intentional in how you show up
and in all that you do. Elevate your
perspective and learn to adjust
it. Emotional struggles will come,
be strong and endure. Be a victor
and never a victim. Embrace failure
as your friend. Push yourself out
of your comfort zone. Connect
with people. Find meaning and
understand your purpose. Listen to
your intuition. Choose your words
wisely.

Love. Love. Love.

Works Cited

Allen, James, 1864-1912. *As a Man Thinketh*. Mount Vernon, N.Y: Peter Pauper Press, 1951.

Rawls, Wilson. *Where the Red Fern Grows*. New York: Bantam Books, 1974.

Frankl, Viktor E. (Viktor Emil), *Man's Search for Meaning: An Introduction to Logotherapy*. Boston: Beacon Press, 1962.

Peirce, Penney, *Frequency*. New York, NY: Astria Books/Beyond Words, 2011.